THE END TO OUR BEGINNING

CHAWANDA J. ALLEN

Because There's More Publishing | Georgia

Copyright © 2017 by Chawanda J. Allen

All rights reserved. This book is protected under the copyright laws of the United States of America. This book or any portion thereof may not be reproduced or used in any manner whatsoever without the express written permission of the publisher except for the use of brief quotations in a book review.

Unless otherwise noted, scripture quotations are taken from the King James Version and New King James Version of the Holy Bible.

ISBN: 979-8-9921977-7-8 (Paperback)
ISBN: 979-8-9921977-6-1 (Hardcover)

Printed in the United States of America.

Published by:
Because There's More Publishing LLC
PO Box 390163
Snellville, GA 30039
becausetheresmorepublishing.com

DEDICATION

This book is dedicated to:

God, my mother (Annie Allen), and my children (Richard and Annah). This book is for the generations who believe God can do anything.

It is God who deserves all the glory for writing this book. It will never be forgotten what He said to me, "This book belongs to Him." These are the teachings and revelations He shared with me. I simply put them in book form to share with you.

As a child, I listened to my mother's prayers countless times. During my tough times, those prayers echoed in my ear and carried me through. The prayers of the righteous do avail much. They follow you throughout your life to bring hope and change. I pray that my children, the next generation, will grasp the Living Word and apply it to fulfill God's plan and purpose for their lives.

ACKNOWLEDGMENTS

It would be a dishonor if I did not thank all who imparted and supported me throughout the years.

My Family

I am grateful to my family who have been my rock throughout this journey. When the storm came and turned everything upside down, having my mom, Lanetta, Tan, Vernon, Gina, and DeWitt by my side made all the difference in the world. My need for love, stability, prayers, and shelter was met by your presence. Thank you!

My Children

To my children, Richard and Annah, I express my sincere thanks for your unconditional love. You are both the best children any mother could ever ask for.

My Extended Family

It would be remiss of me not to thank Terry and William Holloman, and Laura Lee and Will Douglas (His Fish Tank Crew). Thank you for every prophetic word, teaching, impartation, love, prayers, and support.

Pastoral Leadership

Finally, I want to thank Pastor Joyce Terrell and Bishop Leo Lewis for their support. I have witnessed the effects of your teachings and impartations. Your tireless efforts in ministry to fulfill the Father's will are greatly appreciated. I appreciate you laying a solid foundation through the Word of God and prayer.

It was under your pastorate that I developed a love for prayer, boldness in the Spirit, and an openness to receive God's revelation and experience miracles, signs, and wonders. The pieces are coming together and making sense now for God's greater purpose and glory!

It is my prayer that God can use me to be an antidote to others as you both have been to me. May the blessing of the Lord make you all rich and add no sorrow.

INTRODUCTION

"For My thoughts are not your thoughts, Nor are your ways My ways," says the Lord. ⁹ "For as the heavens are higher than the earth, So are My ways higher than your ways, And My thoughts than your thoughts.

¹⁰ "For as the rain comes down, and the snow from heaven, and does not return there, but water the earth, And make it bring forth and bud, That it may give seed to the sower and bread to the eater, ¹¹ So shall My word be that goes forth from My mouth; It shall not return to Me void, But it shall accomplish what I please, And it shall prosper in the thing for which I sent it. *Isaiah 55:8-11*

The Encounter

It is undeniable that God's thoughts and ways are beyond human comprehension. During a time of prayer, I was swept into God's presence. Just as Isaiah's profound experience with God catapulted him into his impactful ministry, my encounter in the presence of God permanently altered my life and ministry.

During the course of my worship, God interrupted and asked, "Do you believe that the serpent walked?" After my answer, "Yes," I was given revelations from God. The words that He spoke were not audible, but I saw them coming into my spirit. It seemed as though time slowed to a crawl during that beautiful encounter. Afterwards, I was still unable to comprehend the true meaning of what had just occurred. However, when I opened my Bible, the words spoke to me. The Lord taught me about the beginning in a way that I had never known. Through His eyes, I could see everything clearly.

The Book

Prior to this encounter, I was at a friend's house worshipping and the Lord spoke to me about a book. He spoke, "You will write *The End to Our Beginning*." As I wrote the title down, I was unclear as to what this book would be about, until now.

The encounter, the revelation was for His book. He wanted to give us the answers to our questions. What was the motivation behind the deception in the Garden? Why was it necessary for the Word to become flesh and dwell among us as the Son of God? How did Jesus' life, death and resurrection restore what man lost in the beginning? What makes the adversary shudder with fear? And so much more. Come take this journey with me, as I share with you what God shared with me in *The End to Our Beginning*.

CONTENTS

Chapter 1   13
In The Beginning
The Place Where It Began

Chapter 2   23
The Adversary
There's a Snake in the Garden

Chapter 3   32
The Fall in the Garden
The Plot and The Deception

Chapter 4   43
The Consequences of Sin
Adam, Eve, and the Serpent

Reflection I   53
Life Application

Contents

Chapter 5   58
The Last Adam: Jesus Christ
The Word Becomes Flesh

Chapter 6   70
The Mission of Jesus Christ
Back to the Garden of Eden

Chapter 7   *87*
He is The End to Our Beginning
All Things New

Reflection II   89
Life Application

Contact Author   104

Chapter 1

In the Beginning
The Place Where it Began
Genesis 1:1 – 2:17

The Genesis

In the beginning God created the heavens and the earth. ² The earth was without form, and void; and darkness was on the face of the deep. And the Spirit of God was hovering over the face of the waters.

³ Then God said, "Let there be light"; and there was light. ⁴ And God saw the light, that it was good; and God divided the light from the darkness. ⁵ God called the light Day, and the darkness He called Night. So the evening and the morning were the first days.

⁶ Then God said, "Let there be a firmament in the midst of the waters, and let it divide the waters from the waters." ⁷ Thus God made the firmament, and divided the waters which were under the firmament from the waters which were above the firmament; and it was so. ⁸ And God called the firmament Heaven. So the evening and the morning were the second day.

⁹ Then God said, "Let the waters under the heavens be gathered together into one place, and let the dry land appear"; and it was so. ¹⁰ And God called the dry land Earth, and the gathering together of the

waters He called Seas. And God saw that it was good.

[11] Then God said, "Let the earth bring forth grass, the herb that yields seed, and the fruit tree that yields fruit according to its kind, whose seed is in itself, on the earth"; and it was so. [12] And the earth brought forth grass, the herb that yields seed according to its kind, and the tree that yields fruit, whose seed is in itself according to its kind. And God saw that it was good. [13] So the evening and the morning were the third day.

[14] Then God said, "Let there be lights in the firmament of the heavens to divide the day from the night; and let them be for signs and seasons, and for days and years; [15] and let them be for lights in the firmament of the heavens to give light on the earth"; and it was so.

[16] Then God made two great lights: the greater light to rule the day, and the lesser light to rule the night. He made the stars also. [17] God set them in the firmament of the heavens to give light on the earth, [18] and to rule over the day and over the night, and to divide the light from the darkness. And God saw that it was good. [19] So the evening and the morning were the fourth day.

[20] Then God said, "Let the waters abound with an abundance of living creatures, and let birds fly above the earth across the face of the firmament of the heavens." [21] So God created great sea creatures and every living thing that moves, with which the waters abounded, according to their kind, and every winged bird according to its kind. And God saw that it was good.

[22] And God blessed them, saying, "Be fruitful and multiply, and fill the waters in the seas, and let birds multiply on the earth." [23] So the evening and the morning were the fifth day.

[24] Then God said, "Let the earth bring forth the living creature according to its kind: cattle and creeping things and beasts of the earth, each according to its kind"; and it was so. [25] And God made the beast of the earth according to its kind, cattle according to its kind, and everything that creeps on the earth according to its kind. And God saw that it was good.

[26] Then God said, "Let Us make man in Our image, according to Our likeness; let them have dominion over the fish of the sea, over the birds of the air, and over the cattle, over all the earth and over every creeping thing that creeps on the earth.

Governance Established

²⁷ So God created man in His own image; in the image of God He created him; male and female He created them. ²⁸ Then God blessed them, and God said to them, "Be fruitful and multiply; fill the earth and subdue it; have dominion over the fish of the sea, over the birds of the air, and over every living thing that moves on the earth."

²⁹ And God said, "See, I have given you every herb that yields seed which is on the face of all the earth, and every tree whose fruit yields seed; to you it shall be for food. ³⁰ Also, to every beast of the earth, to every bird of the air, and to everything that creeps on the earth, in which there is life, I have given every green herb for food"; and it was so. ³¹ Then God saw everything that He had made, and indeed it was very good. So the evening and the morning were the sixth day.

Genesis 2

Thus the heavens and the earth, and all the host of them, were finished. ² And on the seventh day God ended His work which He had done, and He rested on the seventh day from all His work which He had done. ³ Then God blessed the seventh day and sanctified it, because in it He rested from all His work which God had created and made.

The History of How God Formed Man

⁴ This is the history of the heavens and the earth when they were created, in the day that the Lord God made the earth and the heavens, ⁵ before any plant of the field was in the earth and before any herb of the field had grown. For the Lord God had not caused it to rain on the earth, and there was no man to till the ground; ⁶ but a mist went up from the earth and watered the whole face of the ground.

⁷ And the Lord God formed man of the dust of the ground, and breathed into his nostrils the breath of life; and man became a living being.

Life in the Garden of Eden

⁸ The Lord God planted a garden eastward in Eden, and there He put the man whom He had formed. ⁹ And out of the ground the Lord God made every tree grow that is pleasant to the sight and good for food. The tree of life was also in the midst of the garden, and the tree of the knowledge of good and evil.

¹⁰ Now a river went out of Eden to water the garden, and from there it parted and became four riverheads. ¹¹ The name of the first is Pishon; it is the one which

skirts the whole land of Havilah, where there is gold. ¹² And the gold of that land is good. Bdellium and the onyx stone are there. ¹³ The name of the second river is Gihon; it is the one which goes around the whole land of Cush. ¹⁴ The name of the third river is Hiddekel; it is the one which goes toward the east of Assyria. The fourth river is the Euphrates.

The Commandment

¹⁵ Then the Lord God took the man and put him in the garden of Eden to tend and keep it. ¹⁶ And the Lord God commanded the man, saying, "Of every tree of the garden you may freely eat; ¹⁷ but of the tree of the knowledge of good and evil you shall not eat, for in the day that you eat of it you shall surely die."

Life Before the Fall

As a prerequisite to understanding the restorative and redemptive work of Jesus, we must first grasp what Adam and Eve possessed before the Fall.

1. God made Adam and Eve in His image.

Adam and Eve were an earthly reflection of God. Through them, God saw Himself.

2. They were clothed in light.

This is the message which we have heard from Him and declare to you, that God is light and in Him is no darkness at all (1 John 1:5). As God is light (Ps. 104:2), so were Adam and Eve. Their bodies were radiant. Therefore, clothing was not necessary in the Garden of Eden.

3. Glorious Bodies

As Adam and Eve were created in the unblemished Light of the Creator, neither their bodies nor their minds were tainted by the consequences of sin. Thus, their bodies remained undefiled by sickness, disease, death, and other afflictions.

4. A relationship and fellowship with God that was unbroken

God was their constant companion and they enjoyed continuous communion with Him. In His presence, Adam and Eve were completely invincible, unafraid, and unreserved.

5. Innocence

Adam and Eve had only one point of reference: God. Their hands and hearts were pure. Before the fall, their lives were completely free of sin.

6. **No warring in the flesh.**

   Adam and Eve did not wrestle with the internal struggles caused by sin. This is significant because they were free to make their own decisions, yet their immersion in the pure presence of God enabled them to remain undefiled. In other words, Adam and Eve were not aware of the existence of evil. They were created and resided in the presence of God, where the world is uncontaminated and tranquil.

7. **Dominion**

   In God's design, Adam and Eve had dominion - the ability to compel others to obey and subjugate them (Strong's H7287). All living creatures that traveled by air, sea, and land were ruled by them. In the same way that Adam and Eve benefited from God's continuous presence on earth, so did the creatures of the earth.

8. **The Garden of Eden**

   Humanity could not have envisioned a more idyllic place to live with God on earth. As Adam and Eve lived in a pristine environment, God's presence and provision abound. Neither Adam nor Eve lacked anything. In fact, God had provided everything down to the last detail. Each and every good and pleasing thing was at their disposal. Fruitfulness abounded and work was effortless.

9. God's Word

In order to protect Adam and Eve, God gave them His Word. The two of them were not ignorant. As long as they obeyed and did not eat from the Tree of the Knowledge of Good and Evil, they would triumph over their adversary.

Unfortunately, Adam and Eve faced a formidable foe, and life as they had known it was about to end abruptly.

Chapter 2

The Adversary
There's a Snake in The Garden
Genesis 3:1

The Subtle Enemy

Now the serpent was more subtil than any beast of the field which the LORD God had made. *And he said unto the woman, Yea, hath God said, Ye shall not eat of every tree in the garden?* (Genesis 3:1)

The Real Snake in the Garden

Our next chapter introduces us to the serpent, who is described as being subtil, which means crafty, shrewd, sly, sensible, cunning (most often in a negative sense), and prudent (Strong's H6715). Nonetheless, before discussing the serpent in the garden, we must examine the entity who used the serpent to enter the garden and entice Eve. The entity is known as Lucifer.

What was Lucifer's motivation for deceiving mankind? Understanding the why involves understanding who he was and what led to his expulsion from heaven in the first place. Understanding this is at the core of his deception in the garden. First, let's take a look at what the Word of God says about him.

In Isaiah 14:12-15, he is described as the son of the morning who desired to exalt his throne above the stars of God in order to be like Him. However, he was defeated and hurled into hell.

¹² How art thou fallen from heaven, O Lucifer, son of the morning? How art thou cut down to the ground, which didst weaken the nations? ¹³ For thou hast said in thine heart, I will ascend into heaven, I will exalt my throne above the stars of God: I will sit also upon the mount of the congregation, in the sides of the north: ¹⁴ I will ascend above the heights of the clouds; I will be like the most High. ¹⁵ Yet thou shalt be brought down to hell, to the sides of the pit.

Further details of the character of Lucifer are provided in Ezekiel 28:12-17, where he is described as the anointed cherub, a guardian angel, whose ways were perfect until iniquity was found in him. According to the text, his heart was lifted up because of his beauty, and he corrupted (perverted and destroyed) wisdom in pursuit of splendor.

¹² "Son of man, take up a lamentation for the king of Tyre, and say to him, 'Thus says the Lord God: You were the seal of perfection, Full of wisdom and perfect in beauty. ¹³ Thou hast been in Eden the garden of God; every precious stone was thy covering, the sardius, topaz, and the diamond, the beryl, the onyx, and the jasper, the sapphire, the emerald, and the carbuncle, and gold: the workmanship of thy tabrets and of thy pipes was prepared in thee in the day that thou wast created." ¹⁴ Thou art the anointed cherub that covereth; and I have set thee so: thou wast upon the holy mountain of God; thou hast walked up and down in the midst of the stones of fire. ¹⁵ Thou wast perfect in thy ways from the day that thou wast created, till iniquity was found in thee.

¹⁶ By the multitude of thy merchandise they have filled the midst of thee with violence, and thou hast sinned: therefore I will cast thee as profane out of the mountain of God: and I will destroy thee, O covering cherub, from the midst of the stones of fire. ¹⁷ Thine heart was lifted up because of thy beauty, thou hast corrupted thy wisdom by reason of thy brightness: I will cast thee to the ground, I will lay thee before kings, that they may behold thee.

In Luke 10:18, Jesus refers to Satan's fall from heaven.

¹⁸ And He said to them, "I saw Satan fall like lightning from heaven.

When the enemy was expelled from heaven, he fell like lightning. At the moment Satan was falling from heaven, his light was disappearing in mid-air and by the time he hit the ground, he was immersed in total darkness. As a result, the entire earth became enveloped in darkness as well. The light that he once knew was no longer available to him. His existence was spent in obscurity, unable to possess anything, until God began to form and fill the Earth.

From these three passages of scripture, we glean insight into three reasons for his fall.

1. **His heart was lifted up.**

    Lifted up means haughty, proud, exalted, lofty, and arrogant (Strong's H1361). He was full of himself. Proverbs 16:18 warns us that *pride goes before destruction, and a haughty spirit before a fall.*

2. **Iniquity was first found in him.**

    Iniquity means injustice, unrighteousness, unjust, wrong, violent deeds of injustice, evil, perverseness, and wickedness (Strong's H5766). Lucifer was so mesmerized by his own beauty, wisdom, and position that he exalted himself and began to desire the honor and glory due to God alone. He further creates confusion and division in the Kingdom of Heaven with a third of the angels standing with him.

God is not the author of confusion (1 Cor. 14:33) and a house divided against itself cannot stand (Mt.12:25). Lucifer solidified his eviction when we wickedly sought to divide and conquer. Evil cannot dwell with God. Psalm 5:4 declares that *God does not take pleasure in wickedness, nor shall evil dwell with Him.*

3. **He wanted to be God.**

    There's only one Sovereign, true and living God. Isaiah 46:9 reads, *For I am God, and there is no other; I am God, and there is none like Me.* Exodus 20:3 states, *You shall have no other gods before Me.* Lucifer's attempt to assert himself as a god encapsulated his treachery and defilement. God looked upon him as a profane thing.

The Result of Trading Truth for Lies

Did Lucifer really believe he had any possibility of overthrowing God's power? The mere idea is insane. He grossly deceived himself, trading wisdom for self-induced lies and notions of grandeur. As a result, he is now called the Father of Lies. The angels who chose to believe and follow him only contributed to his delusion. Their belief and support reinforced his madness.

When you believe in something, you give it power.

He was gaining power from their belief, and it only served to make his heart haughtier and more prideful. His fall was imminent. He and a third of the angels were suddenly kicked out of heaven.

Revelations 12:7-9 *And war broke out in heaven: Michael and his angels fought with the dragon; and the dragon and his angels fought, but they did not prevail, nor was a place found for them in heaven any longer. So the great dragon was cast out, that serpent of old, called the Devil and Satan, who deceives the whole world; he was cast to the earth, and his angels were cast out with him.*

Now expelled, their rights were revoked, which resulted in the loss of heavenly authority, position, and name. The Bible only mentions Lucifer by name one time and that's in connection to his fall in Isaiah 14:12. Otherwise he's simply called Satan, which means adversary, opponent, one who withstands, and archenemy of good (Strong's H7854). He is also known as the devil, which means false accuser, slanderer, calumniator, traducer (Strong's G1228). The fallen angels are commonly called devils or demons, which means evil spirits or the messengers and ministers of the devil (Strong's G1140).

The Tradeoff is Permanent

Sin is costly and no one is more aware of that truth than the adversary and the fallen angels. There is no forgiveness or remission of sins for Satan and his gang. There's no appealing to the courts of heaven for mercy. The judgment for their insurrection and rebellion is permanent (2 Peter 2:4, Jude 1:6). Their fate is sealed, and an eternal fire has been prepared for them (Mt. 25:41, Rev. 20:10).

> *Be sober, be vigilant; because your adversary the devil walks about like a roaring lion, seeking whom he may devour. - 1 Peter 5:8*

Be Sober, Be Vigilant

Satan has nothing else to lose. He's already lost everything. He comes as a son of the morning, pretending to be an angel of light (2 Cor. 11:14), but he's full of darkness. Nothing about him is good. The entirety of his mission is to steal, kill and destroy the very creature made in God's image and likeness - humanity (John 10:10a). He doesn't want us to walk in our identity as children of God. He doesn't want us to exercise our authority on earth. Instead, he wants us to do what he did - trade the truth for lies.

As we will see in the next chapter, the adversary doesn't play fair.

- He is patient and methodical in his pursuit.
- He will study your likes and dislikes, beliefs and doubts about God and yourself, strengths and weaknesses, convictions, and insecurities, what you value and devalue; and attempt to use this info to his advantage.
- He will present something that looks good as bait to lead you down a road to destruction. Every good-looking thing is not a God thing, and neither is every worldly or material gain a blessing from God.

He will do whatever he can and use whoever he can to carry out his plan. The good news is that God has given us power to overcome the enemy of our souls, beginning with His Word. The Word was enough in the Garden, and it is enough for believers now. But as it was with Adam and Eve, the choice to obey is ours.

Chapter 3

The Fall
The Plot and The Deception
Genesis 3:1-6

Unsuspecting Humanity

Now the serpent was more subtil than any beast of the field which the LORD God had made. And he said unto the woman, Yea, hath God said, Ye shall not eat of every tree of the garden?

² And the woman said unto the serpent, We may eat of the fruit of the trees of the garden: ³ But of the fruit of the tree which is in the midst of the garden, God hath said, Ye shall not eat of it, nor shall ye touch it, lest ye die.

⁴ And the serpent said unto the woman, Ye shall not surely die: ⁵ For God doth know that in the day ye eat thereof, then your eyes shall be opened, and ye shall be as gods, knowing good and evil.

⁶ And when the woman saw that the tree was good for food, and that it was pleasant to the eyes, and a tree to be desired to make one wise, she took of the fruit thereof, and did eat, and gave also unto her husband with her; and he did eat.

The Plot

God created man (male and female) in His image and likeness and bestowed upon them something the adversary so desperately desired during his attempt to overthrow God's rule in Heaven but lost – a kingdom to rule. In addition to the earth, God also granted man dominion over every creature roaming the air, sea, and land. This included Satan and the fallen angels as well. According to Ezekiel 28:17, Lucifer was cast down to the earth or land when he was expelled from heaven (Strong's H776).

Furthermore, God made man from the ground Satan was cast down upon and gave man the power to subjugate him. His hatred was further fueled by the resemblance between man and the Father. It was as if every time he looked at man, he saw God and he was reminded of everything he had lost.

At some point in the plot, the enemy devises a plan to deceive man. If he were to successfully convince mankind to trade the truth for the lie, the fallout would be as follows:

1. Man's Death

The ultimate objective was not so much to kill the human being physically, as it was to destroy him spiritually. The adversary recognized through his own experience that sin could permanently separate man from God. Thus, sin is the avenue he uses to control, operate through, and access the rights of man.

2. His Freedom from Man's Rule

Satan needed for man to be out of position, in order to maneuver unopposed in the earth.

It is important to note that as long as you are not opposing Satan's kingdom, he doesn't care if you go to church, perform miracles, preach the gospel, do good works, etc. Sons and daughters of God who recognize their identity and walk in their God-given authority pose the biggest threat to the kingdom of darkness.

3. Access to Man

Man's only point of reference prior to the fall was God who is good. The knowledge of evil would present another point of reference, Satan. Man would now have a choice to follow good or evil.

The Target

In this case, the adversary identifies his target as the woman. He waits and examines the situation for the right moment to make his move.

The Deception

The enemy relies on the same cognitive process that was responsible for his fall - presuming that he is God. In order to achieve success, Satan needed for Eve to doubt God's Word and question her identity. Consider the passage carefully.

Genesis 3:1 *Now the serpent was more cunning than any beast of the field which the Lord God had made. And he said to the woman, "Has God indeed said, 'You shall not eat of every tree of the garden'?"*

Let us begin by asking why the adversary chose the woman over Adam? After study of the scriptures, I believe his approach is attributed to two factors:

1. **This command was given to Adam, not Eve (Genesis 2:16-17).**

In his role as Eve's husband, Adam was responsible for ensuring he clearly explained God's instructions to her. Unfortunately, when a message is received by one person and then relayed to another, it is possible for important details to be lost in transmission. Genesis 3:2-3 reveals that the woman omitted important details that exposed a misinterpretation of the commandment.

2. Eve's ability to influence Adam.

The dictionary defines influence as the ability or power of persons, objects, or events to affect, direct, or determine the actions, feelings, opinions, etc., of others (Dictionary.com). If the adversary is successful in convincing the woman to consume the fruit, she will serve as a powerful temptation for Adam. After all, she was his wife. Consequently, Satan planned to exploit her relationship with Adam to influence him to disobey God.

Secondly, let's address the obvious. **For what purpose does the woman converse with the serpent?** I believe that Adam and the woman communicated regularly with the animals in the garden. Keep in mind that God gave Adam the assignment to name the animals (Genesis 2:19), in addition to giving him and Eve dominion over all living creatures on earth as well as in the air, sea, and land (Gen. 1:17-28). God created us to operate in the realm of the supernatural. This dialogue furthers confirms the power we possessed in God. And through Christ, we can operate in the supernatural power of God now!

What was Satan's purpose in using the serpent?

The scripture provides a clue. It says in the text that he (the serpent) was "more subtil than any beast of the field." Subtil is synonymous with subtle, shrewd, cunning, and intelligent (Strong's H6175). Essentially, it speaks to the serpent's wisdom and credibility. It was imperative for the adversary to use a creature that could influence the woman. Perhaps, one with whom she had conversed with in the past and had her ear. In the same way Satan possibly thought about his own fall, and how the fallen angels were impressed by his beauty and wisdom, and willingly embraced his lies. Since it worked before, why not try it again? The same tactics, just a different setting and subject matter.

Finally, notice the wording of the question, "hath God said, Ye shall not eat of every tree of the garden?" Here, Satan intentionally twists God's Word. While he was well aware of the tree God had forbidden them to eat from, the question he had to answer was whether or not she was aware. Therefore, he begins the conversation with this leading question in order to guide the exchange in the desired direction.

Genesis 3:2-3 *And the woman said unto the serpent, We may eat of the fruit of the trees of the garden: But of the fruit of the tree which is in the midst of* *the garden, God hath said, Ye shall not eat of it, neither shall ye touch it, lest ye die.*

The woman's response exposes a few cracks in her understanding and the adversary uses that his advantage.

1. **First, she didn't name the tree.** Eve simply says the tree in the midst of the garden.

The problem with this response is that there are two trees situated amidst the garden, namely, the Tree of Life and the Tree of the Knowledge of Good and Evil (Genesis 2:9). What tree is she referring to?

2. **Secondly, she says something God never said, "neither shall ye touch it."** It could be argued that Adam did not relay the command verbatim, or that further clarification is necessary.

Unfortunately, the adversary embodying the serpent becomes her voice of clarity and reasoning.

Genesis 3:4-5 *Then the serpent said to the woman, "You will not surely die. For God knows that in the day you eat of it your eyes will be opened, and you will be like God, knowing good and evil."*

In a self-assured manner, he takes advantage of the opportunity and inserts his lies. Despite this, the text contains a risky assumption made by the adversary that could have backfired on him as well. The adversary assumes that she doesn't know who she is. The woman had nothing to desire because she was already like God, made in His image and likeness (Genesis 1:26-27). Nevertheless, she finds the proposition of her adversary appealing (which exposes an identity issue) and chooses to consume it. In turn, she gives the fruit to Adam, who consumes it as well.

Genesis 3:6 *So when the woman saw that the tree was good for food, that it was pleasant to the eyes, and a tree desirable to make one wise, she took of its fruit and ate. She also gave to her husband with her, and he ate.*

The Trade Off

God's instructions to Adam and Eve established an important boundary which, if obeyed, would ensure their safety. God's Word doesn't preclude us from living a fulfilled life. On the contrary, Jesus came so that we might have life and that more abundantly (John 10:10b). His Word affords us protection when followed. If followed, His Word would have prevented man's fall and the ensuing battle of choosing between God, who is good, and the devil, who is evil. Thankfully, God is intimately aware of the adversary and knows what we need to overcome him and live victoriously in the earth today.

Missed Opportunities

While they conversed, the woman was given numerous opportunities to uphold God's command and silence the serpent, but she continued to entertain his lies. Please note that the consumption of the lie preceded the eating of the fruit. Consequently, her eyes were opened to see what the adversary wanted her to see. As individuals, we should be cautious of the words we entertain as they may lead us down a path that God did not intend for us. The adversary recognizes the power of a seed. As the seed germinated in the soil of Eve's mind, he simply waited for that fruit to come forth.

The Scriptures do not describe any dialogue between Adam and the woman. It only discloses that she provides him with fruit, which he eats. This illustrates the importance and power of influence. Satan does not play by the rules. He will use anyone available, especially those who are close or are in close proximity to us. Adam received a direct word from God, but now he looks at the woman he loves, and nothing appears to have happened to her, and he eats.

Danger Zone

It's dangerous to base your decision on whether or not to obey God, on the consequences or lack thereof someone else has faced. Humans are not our litmus test for how we should live, the Word of God is. What did God say to Adam? In that moment, Adam had the power to rebuke and exert his authority over the serpent/adversary, but he chose not to. Instead, he disobeys God and, by default, allows the adversary access to the earth he was created to rule. The adversary emerges now as the "ruler of the world" (John 12:31) and as the "prince of the power of the air" (Ephesians 2:2).

The Weight of Accountability

Due to Adam's receipt of the command, he bears a greater responsibility for his behavior. In the next chapter, we will see that nothing happened until Adam consumed the fruit. Now, God moves to address the sin in the Garden, just as he moved to address the sin in heaven with Lucifer and the fallen angels.

Chapter 4

The Consequences of Sin
Adam, Eve, and the Serpent
Genesis 3:8-24

God Confronts Adam and the Woman

And they heard the sound of the Lord God walking in the garden in the cool [afternoon breeze] of the day, so the man and his wife hid and kept themselves hidden from the presence of the Lord God among the trees of the garden. [9] But the Lord God called to Adam, and said to him, "Where are you?"

[10] He said, "I heard the sound of You [walking] in the garden, and I was afraid because I was naked; so I hid myself." [11] God said, "Who told you that you were naked? Have you eaten [fruit] from the tree of which I commanded you not to eat?"
[12] And the man said, "The woman whom You gave to be with me—she gave me [fruit] from the tree, and I ate it."

[13] Then the Lord God said to the woman, "What is this that you have done?" And the woman said, "The serpent beguiled and deceived me, and I ate [from the forbidden tree]." (Genesis 3:8-13)

Sin at Work

Immediately in this passage, we see the consequences of sin. The adversary loves to make sin appealing, but he fails to disclose its effects are long-term and far-reaching.

1. **Shame and Condemnation** - aware of their misdeeds, they try to avoid God.

2. **Distorted Image - their reflection has been tainted by sin.** The reflection of God is no longer intact.

3. **Corruptible bodies** - their bodies are now subject to death. As a result of sin, death entered the world (Romans 5:12-14).

4. **Nakedness** – there is no longer a covering of light over them, and they are forced to confront their own nakedness.

5. **Fear** – they were terrified of God, not in an awe-inspiring or reverent sense, but in a truly dreadful manner.

6. **Blame-shifting** – rather than be accountable and take responsibility for their own choices, Adam and the woman allocate blame to someone else.

7. **Innocence Lost** – the knowledge of evil has been imparted to them.

God is now called upon to deal with the sin in the Garden and He begins with the serpent.

The Serpent is Cursed

Genesis 3:14 -15 *And the LORD God said unto the serpent, Because thou hast done this, thou art cursed above all cattle, and above every beast of the field; upon thy belly shalt thou go, and dust shalt thou eat all the days of thy life: And I will put enmity between thee and the woman, and between thy seed and her seed; it shall bruise thy head, and thou shalt bruise his heel.*

The term "cursed" is introduced for the first time in the Bible. According to Strong's, the primitive root word means to bitterly curse or execrate (Strong's H779). By definition, execrate means to declare to be evil or detestable.

As a result of his deceptive works:

- Once admired, the serpent is now loathed over all other animals in the field.
- The animal moved from walking upright to crawling on its belly.
- It was sentenced to live on dust for the remainder of its life.
- There will be hostility and hatred between the seed of the serpent and the seed of the woman.

- As a result of the seed of the woman, its head will be crushed.

The Woman's Punishment

Genesis 3:16 *Unto the woman he said, I will greatly multiply thy sorrow and thy conception; in sorrow thou shalt bring forth children; and thy desire shall be to thy husband, and he shall rule over thee.*

As a result of the woman's disobedience:

- When conceiving and giving birth, she would experience sorrow (pain, labor, hardship, and toil).
- Her husband will be the one she desires and longs for.
- Her husband will rule over her.

Let me pause here for a minute. As shared earlier, when God created man (male and female) He gave them both dominion or authority to govern the earth and everything that traveled by air, sea, and land. However, God gave Adam the assignment to name the animals, which he had dominion over. You will notice that it wasn't until after the fall that Adam names his wife, Eve.

And Adam called his wife's name Eve; because she was the mother of all living. Genesis 3:20

Initially, she was simply called Woman – the female version of Adam (Gen. 2:23). I believe the name change was indicative of the fact that Eve would now be subject to her husband. For clarity, God was establishing family order, not giving a license to the husband to devalue, neglect or abuse the wife. Ephesians 5:22-25 states it this way:

> *Wives, submit to your own husbands, as to the Lord. For the husband is head of the wife, as also Christ is head of the church; and He is the Savior of the body. Therefore, just as the church is subject to Christ, so let the wives be to their own husbands in everything.*

Ultimately, the husband would be responsible for and carry the weight of leading the family. Had Adam led in the Garden and adhered to God's command, the outcome may have been different for humanity. In the end, it was Adam's disobedience to God's Word that ultimately led to the fall of man and sin's entrance into the world. Now, Adam has to face the repercussions of his disobedience.

Therefore, just as through one man sin entered the world, and death through sin, and thus death spread to all men, because all sinned.
Romans 5:12

Adam's Punishment

Genesis 3:17-19 *Then to Adam He said, "Because you have heeded the voice of your wife, and have eaten from the tree of which I commanded you, saying, 'You shall not eat of it': "Cursed is the ground for your sake; In toil you shall eat of it all the days of your life. Both thorns and thistles it shall bring forth for you, And you shall eat the herb of the field. In the sweat of your face you shall eat bread till you return to the ground, For out of it you were taken; For dust you are*, And to dust you shall return."

As a result of Adam's disobedience:

- The ground is cursed for his sake. Both the earth and animals are experiencing the effects of Adam's sin.
- He will eat the fruit of the ground in sorrow (pain, labor, hardship, and toil).
- He will have to labor hard to produce and contend with thorns and thistles.

- Death entered the world. He would return to the dust from which he was taken.

You will notice that God does not "curse" Adam and Eve for their disobedience. He uses that term only in reference to the serpent and the ground. I believe God strategically and purposefully chose not to curse what He had already blessed in Genesis 1:28 and purposed to restore.

So God created man in His own image; in the image of God He created him; male and female He created them. **Then God blessed them**...
(Genesis 1:27-28)

Nevertheless, man had to be judged for their disobedience and the ripple effect of sin continues to permeate throughout generations. Having said that, Adam/Eve's fall was no surprise to God. He had already purposed a remedy for the calamity that had now befallen man.

Removal from the Garden of Eden

Genesis 3:22-24 *And the LORD God said, Behold, the man is become as one of us, to know good and evil: and now, lest he put forth his hand, and take also of the tree of life, and eat, and live forever:*

*Therefore the L*ORD *God sent him forth from the garden of Eden, to till the ground from whence he was taken. So he drove out the man; and he placed at the east of the garden of Eden Cherubims, and a flaming sword which turned every way, to keep the way of the tree of life.*

Now that man had become as God and the angels, to know good and evil, the conflict on who to serve now comes into play. There's God who is good and Satan who is evil. Unknowingly, their knowledge of evil also made them susceptible to it. God could not allow them to remain in the Garden with access to the Tree of Life. To do so, would doom them to live perpetually in a fallen state. In essence, they would be like Satan and his imps – eternally doomed without any hope of redemption. They had to leave. It was necessary for God's plan of salvation.

What the Adversary Didn't See Coming

The adversary's plan seemed to work.

- He got kicked out of Heaven. Adam and Eve got kicked out of the Garden of Eden.
- He lost his position and authority. Adam and Eve lost their position and negated their dominion in the earth.

- He had no recourse for redemption. There was no forgiveness of sin for him. In fact, he's already been judged and condemned. However, he wrongly assumed that man would suffer the same fate.

What the adversary didn't see coming was God's plan of salvation to reconcile man back to Himself and to restore to man that which was lost in the garden. What he thought was the end, actually set the stage for a new beginning through Christ Jesus.

Reflections I

Life Application

1. God's Word to Adam and Eve established an important boundary and provided protection against the adversary. How does God's Word help us to overcome today?

2. Why was the adversary effective in deceiving Eve? Adam? What were some of the tactics he employed? How can we guard against those same devices today?

3. What were your takeaways from chapters 1 - 4 and how can you apply them to your life today?

_____
_____
_____
_____
_____
_____
_____
_____
_____
_____
_____
_____
_____
_____
_____
_____
_____

> *My word that goes out from My mouth - it will not return to Me unfulfilled; but it will accomplish what I intend, and cause to succeed what I sent it to do.*
>
> Isaiah 55:10-11 CJB

Chapter 5

The Last Adam: Jesus Christ
The Word Becomes Flesh
John 1:1-14

The Word Becomes Flesh

In the beginning was the Word, and the Word was with God, and the Word was God. ²He was in the beginning with God. ³All things were made through Him, and without Him nothing was made that was made. ⁴ In Him was life, and the life was the light of men. ⁵And the light shines in the darkness, and the darkness did not comprehend it.

⁶ There was a man sent from God, whose name was John. ⁷ This man came for a witness, to bear witness of the Light, that all through him might believe. ⁸ He was not that Light, but was sent to bear witness of that Light. ⁹ That was the true Light which gives light to every man coming into the world.

¹⁰ He was in the world, and the world was made through Him, and the world did not know Him. ¹¹ He came to His own, and His own did not receive Him. ¹² But as many as received Him, to them He gave the right to become children of God, to those who believe in His name: ¹³ who were born, not of blood, nor of the will of the flesh, nor of the will of man, but of God.

¹⁴ And the Word became flesh and dwelt among us, and we beheld His glory, the glory as of the only begotten of the Father, full of grace and truth.

The Word is the Answer

The Word has always been an integral part of God's plan for humankind, as He and His Word are one. According to John 1:1, *the Word was with God and was God.* Upon creating the heavens and the earth, God spoke the Word. God gave Adam and Eve the Word in order to safeguard them in the Garden. Moreover, the potency and efficacy of God's Word continue to be evident in our lives today.

Attributes of the Word	**Scripture**
Endures forever, imperishable	1 Pet. 1:23,25, Is. 40:8, Mt. 24:35, Ps. 119:89
Living and active	Heb. 4:12
Full of power	Heb. 4:12
Sharper than a two-edged sword, Sword of the Spirit	Heb. 4:12, Eph. 6:17
Judges the thoughts and attitudes of the heart	Heb. 4:12
Will not return void	Is. 34:16
Flawless	Ps. 12:6
Activates and increases faith	Rom. 10:17
Plantable	Jas 1:21
Builds up	Acts 20:32
Lights the way	Ps. 119:105
Truth	Ps. 119:11
Spirit and life	John 6:63
Liberates and sets free	John 8:32
Power of God to Salvation	Rom. 1:16

It's so befitting that the instrument God would use to undo what the first man, Adam, did in the Garden, would be His Word. The Word was and is the one thing God could count on to not return to Him void of accomplishing the mission (Isaiah 34:16). But for His plan to work, the Word had to become flesh.

The Need for a Man

In order to fulfill the promise concerning the coming of Jesus in the Scriptures, it was imperative for the Word to become a man. Prophets throughout the Old Testament prophesied about Him, while types and shadows in the Word divulged Him. As early as Genesis 3:15, when God declares the head of the serpent will be bruised by the Seed of the woman to Isaiah 7:14 which foreshadows His virgin birth, the Word was out and its manifestation was imminent.

It is important to reflect on God's love for mankind before I continue any further. The depth of God's love for His creation is beyond comprehending. It's absolutely mind-blowing when one really reflects on the actions God took to redeem man. Even more astonishing is that He would implement a plan where a man was necessary, considering the first Adam messed up so badly. I believe God is saying to His sons in this moment - you are redeemable. Regardless of how far you have fallen, how grave your mistake, or how far you may have thought you were from God's reach, God's love for you has not changed! In addition, His provision of a path for man to return to Him beautifully illustrates His love for us then and now.

Our study of God's efforts to redeem mankind can proceed now that we have reflected on His love. In a very practical sense, the Word becoming flesh would allow Jesus to experience our weakness and temptations, even though He was without sin.

As a man, Jesus...	Scripture
grew and developed	Luke 2:52
was baptized	Mt. 3:13
received affirmation	Mt. 3:17
was tempted	Mt. 4:1-8, Heb. 4:15
cried	John 11:35, Lk. 19:41
had to deny His will	Luke 22:42
humbled Himself and walked in obedience to God	Phil. 2:8
fasted and prayed	Mt. 4:1-11, John 17
suffered at the hands of man	Mt. 20:17-19
was betrayed	Mt. 26:47-49
felt forsaken	Mt. 27:46
was honored	Mt. 21:1-11
was arrested, tried, and sentenced to death	Mt. 26:47-55
experienced victory	John 20:1-10

Although his experiences mirrored some of our own, He did not sin. Consequently, His obedience provided the entrance for many to become righteous, which is in stark contrast with the first Adam who made many sinners through his disobedience (Rom. 5:19).

First Man - Adam	Last Adam - Jesus
Old Man	New Man
Disobedient	Obedient
Self Will	God's Will
Subject to Death	Power over Death
Living Being	Life-Giving Spirit
Earth Man	Lord from Heaven
Lost Dominion	Regained Dominion
Sinful	Sinless
Wounded for Woman	Wounded for Humanity
Unrighteous	Righteous
Banned from the Tree of Life	He is the Tree of Life
Covered His Sin	Covered Our Sins
Kicked out of the Garden	Received into Heaven
Separated from God	One with God
Brought Judgment	Brought Salvation
Offered Sacrifices	Was the Perfect Sacrifice
Yielded to Temptation	Resisted Temptation
Forfeited His Destiny	Fulfilled His Mission
Gave Up His Birth Right	Heir of All Things

The Need for a Woman

The Word could not become flesh without the womb of the woman. God created the world so that everything would produce after its own kind, including man. By divine predestination, the woman was to be the vehicle through which the entire human race was released into the earth. According to the Scriptures, this is why Eve is considered the mother of all living as she was the first vessel to give birth to human life on earth.

Considering Eve's failure in the Garden, I find it fascinating that God would design a plan that required a woman. In this moment, I believe God is declaring to His daughters as He did for His sons - you are redeemable. God has always been mindful of us and we've always played a significant role in His plans. We have purpose and promise! There is no diminishing of God's love for us. He loves us through our accomplishments and our mistakes. The fact that He would include the woman and give her such an integral role in His plan of salvation attests to His unending love for us then and now.

Bringing it all Together

The generations anticipated the coming of Messiah and now it was time to reveal the woman who would give birth to Him. In this very special undertaking, God chose Mary as the surrogate. At the time, she was engaged to Joseph, a descendant of King David.

Mary's virginity and Joseph's royal lineage were both prophesied in the Old Testament (Isaiah 7:14, 9:6-7).

During my study of these two individuals, I became intrigued by the meaning of their names. Joseph is defined as "let him add" in the Greek (Strong's G2501), whereas Mary is defined as "their rebellion" (Strong's G137). I believe their names are prophetic and speaks to God's plan to add back to man what was lost in the garden due to man's rebellion. Furthermore, God deems Mary to be worthy and highly favored in spite of her name (Luke 1:28).

No matter what name or label man has given you, God has already counted you worthy of His redemptive work. He's just waiting on your response. It is sufficient for you to believe, accept, and submit to what Jesus has already done and provided for you.

Let's examine Joseph and Mary's response.

Their Response

As Joseph and Mary came under the direction of God, they took the path Adam and Eve did not take in the Garden - trusting God's Word and submitting to His will (Matthew 1:18-25, Luke 1:27-38).

Matthew 1:24-25 *Then Joseph being raised from sleep did as the angel of the Lord had bidden him, and took unto him his wife: And knew her not till she had brought forth her firstborn son: and he called his name Jesus.*

Luke 1:38 *And Mary said, Behold the handmaid of the Lord; be it unto me according to thy word. And the angel departed from her.*

Their submission to the will of the Father was a pivotable moment in history - both personally and for humanity as a whole. In essence, what was about to happen in Mary's womb would alter the course of our lives forever.

The Manifestation

It is by God's supernatural provision that the seed (His Word) and the activator (His Spirit) are provided for an immaculate conception. Upon completion of the gestation period, the word of God is fulfilled and manifested in the flesh.

Son of God
Son of Man
Immanuel – God with Us
Wonderful Counselor
Mighty God
Everlasting Father
Redeemer
Lamb of God
Prince of Peace
Author and Finisher of Our Faith
Chief Cornerstone
Light of the World
Bread of Life
The Christ
The Word
Resurrection and the Life
True Vine
Mediator Between God and Man
Our Advocate
Alpha and Omega
Lion of the Tribe of Judah
Root of David
Head of the Church
The Bright and Morning Star
Great High Priest

The Deliverer
Faithful and True
The Way, The Truth, The Life
Good Shepherd
The Tree of Life
Lord of All
King of kings
The Messiah
Our Hope
God Manifested in the Flesh
The Gift of God
The Holy One
Savior of the World
Jesus is born.

Let Joseph and Mary serve as an example to us. Our obedience to God has the ability to not only impact our lives in a very powerful and meaningful way, but generations to follow. Let us be encouraged to trust and submit to the will of God and go all the way with Him into eternity.

Chapter 6

The Mission of Jesus Christ:
Back to the Garden

Jesus' ministry on earth – His conception, life, death, burial, resurrection, and ascension, serves to reveal God's love and plan of salvation to all who will believe. Through the Word of God, we can gain a clear understanding of Jesus' mission.

- Seek out and save what was lost. Luke 19:10
- Redeem those under the law so that we can acquire adoption as sons. Gal. 4:5
- Salvation from sin for His people. Mt. 1:2.
- To serve. Mt. 20:28, Mark 10:45
- Give His life as a ransom for many. Mt. 20:28
- To die for ungodly people. Rom. 5:6
- Make atonement or be a propitiation for our sins. 1 John. 2:2, 4:10, Heb. 2:17-18
- Remove the sin of the world. John 1:29
- To testify to the truth. John 18:37
- Preach the kingdom of God. Luke 4:43
- To restore the brokenhearted. Luke 4:18
- Proclaim liberty to the captives. Luke 4:18
- Recover sight for those who are blind. Luke 4:18
- To liberate those who have been oppressed. Luke 4:18

- To destroy the works of the devil. 1 John 3:8
- Render powerless the devil. Heb. 2:14-15
- To know the only true God. John 17:23
- Destroy the devil who had the power of death through the death of Jesus Christ. Heb. 2:14
- Free those who were subject to slavery due to fear of death. Heb. 2:15
- To give us life and that more abundantly. John 10:10
- To grant eternal life to all who believe in Him. John 6:38-40
- Give us access to the Father in one Spirit. Eph. 2:17-19
- Justification of life for all men. Rom. 5:17-18
- Make the church holy and blameless, by sanctifying her and presenting her without spot or wrinkle. Eph. 5:25-27
- To fulfill the Father's will and accomplish His work. John 4:34, Luke 2:49
- Fulfill the law and the Prophets. Mt. 5:17
- Give light to man. John 1:9
- To provide a way back to the Father. John 14:5-14

- Redeem us from the curse of the law. Gal. 3:13
- Give us the right to become children of God. John 1:12
- Provided a means for reconciling God and humanity. Heb. 2:17
- Make us a new man. 1 Cor. 5:17

Prior to Jesus beginning His earthly ministry, a number of significant events had to occur. Each of these events were integral to the plan of salvation.

Water Baptism (Mt. 3:13-16)

The first event is His baptism by John the Baptist. Water baptism is both a command and a public declaration of our faith in Jesus. It identifies us with the burial and resurrection of Jesus Christ. Symbolically, it represents the burial of our old man and the rebirth of our new life in Christ. Despite the fact that Jesus was not a sinner, he humbled himself in order to identify with those whose sins He would bear.

The Baptism of the Holy Spirit (Mt. 3:16)

The second event was the Spirit of God descending like a dove and settling on Him. The Holy Spirit is necessary for living this life in the manner God intended. His power enables us to be witnesses in the earth for Christ (Acts 1:8).

God's Acceptance & Affirmation (Mt. 3:17)

Jesus was publicly affirmed by God in the third event. The Father affirms the identity of Jesus as His beloved Son and declares His approval and acceptance of Him. For believers, being affirmed by God in our identity as sons and daughters is crucial. The adversary will come to tempt us, as he did with Eve and now Jesus.

The Temptation (Mt. 4:1-11)

Having received affirmation from God, Jesus is led into the wilderness by the Holy Spirit to encounter Satan, who interrupted the destiny of the First Adam in the Garden.

Some contend that Jesus was tempted at His weakest moment, but I disagree. His Spirit was strong, although His flesh was weak from fasting. Contrary to what Satan may have thought, this encounter will not end as the first. With every temptation, Jesus captures a new dimension and regains the dominion man lost in the Garden. Let us examine this passage.

The 1st Dimension (vs. 1-4)

¹Then Jesus was led up by the Spirit into the wilderness to be tempted by the devil. ²And when He had fasted forty days and forty nights, afterward He was hungry. ³Now when the tempter came to Him, he said, "If You are the Son of God, command that these stones become bread."

⁴But He answered and said, "It is written, 'Man shall not live by bread alone, but by every word that proceeds from the mouth of God.' "

Initially, Satan challenges Jesus' identity with a proposition, "If you are the Son of God." However, he is aware of who Jesus is. After all, the Father publicly acknowledged Him (Mt. 3:17). Through his probing, Satan sought to ascertain whether Jesus believed the Father. This was the same method by which he enticed Eve. Eve didn't recognize she was already like God, and thus ate the fruit. In this passage, Satan attempts to entice Jesus into proving He is the Son of God by commanding the stones to become bread. Satan understood that as the Son of God, Jesus possessed the same power to speak a thing and see it manifest. Afterall, Jesus is the Word manifested in the flesh (John 1:14).

However, Satan wrongly assumes that enticing Jesus to satisfy a natural need will lead Him to succumb to the temptation. Although this tactic may have worked in the past with others, it did not work with Jesus. Instead, Jesus defeats Satan with the Word and takes dominion over the natural realm.

If you find yourself needing to prove who you are, check your heart's motivation and ask God to heal you in that area.

The 2ⁿᵈ Dimension (vs. 5-7)

⁵Then the devil took Him up into the holy city, set Him on the pinnacle of the temple, ⁶and said to Him, "If You are the Son of God, throw Yourself down. For it is written: 'He shall give His angels charge over you,' and, 'In their hands they shall bear you up, Lest you dash your foot against a stone.' "
⁷Jesus said to him, "It is written again, 'You shall not tempt the Lord your God.' "

With the second temptation, the location shifts. Jesus is taken by Satan to the temple's pinnacle (highest point). Again, he challenges Jesus' identity and attempts to manipulate Him with the Word. He hopes that Jesus will respond outside of God's will in order to prove that He is the Son of God.

Manipulating scripture for personal gain is not new to Satan. In Genesis 3, he used a similar strategy on Eve. The fact that he inserts the Word and the setting is the temple in the Holy City is by no means a coincidence. Both represent that which is spiritual. Consequently, Jesus responds with the Word, defeats Satan, and takes dominion over the spiritual realm.

When you belong to God, you don't have to prove who you are. Submit to God and allow Him to do the revealing.

The 3rd Dimension (vs. 8-11)

⁸Again, the devil took Him up on an exceedingly high mountain, and showed Him all the kingdoms of the world and their glory. ⁹And he said to Him, "All these things I will give You if You will fall down and worship me."

¹⁰Then Jesus said to him, "Away with you, Satan! For it is written, 'You shall worship the Lord your God, and Him only you shall serve.' " ¹¹Then the devil left Him, and behold, angels came and ministered to Him.

For the final temptation, Satan takes Jesus up to a high mountain and offers Him all the kingdoms of the world. In this case, the kingdoms of the world would become His (Rev.11:15). Jesus defeats him with the Word of God and regains all power in heaven and earth. Unknowingly, Satan has just made it possible for Jesus to do to him, what he did to man – regain full dominion over the earth - sea, land, and air. Accordingly, the higher Satan took Jesus, the more Jesus defeated him with the Word, and with every temptation Jesus reclaimed territory for us. The entire process was the work of God.

Satan got played. It was a setup.

The benefits that were lost in the Garden as a result of sin have now been restored. The dominion that man lost in the Garden was not only reclaimed by Jesus, but He also gained dominion over sin for us. Now through Jesus, we have redemption through His blood and forgiveness of sins (Eph. 1:7).

Jesus' Ministry

The plan for salvation is evident in the lives of the people Jesus encountered, ministered to, and discipled throughout His ministry.

The judgment pronounced on man in the Garden is undone through His ministry, which involves interaction with the people. Additionally, Jesus came not only to save, but to bless the people and bring about a new testament under the dispensation of grace. The following paragraphs provide an overview of the punishment Adam and Eve received in the Garden, along with some examples of how Jesus has now come to bless and restore the life of all who will receive Him.

Adam

__The Judgment (Gen. 3:17-19)__ **-** He would have to labor and toil to produce.

__The Blessing (Luke 5:4-6):__ While Peter was wrapping up his unfruitful fishing venture, Jesus appears and instructs him to let down his net. At first, he pushes back. But then, he considers who is speaking and follows Jesus' instructions. The resulting catch was more than he could handle.

This blessing was a direct result of his obedience to the instructions of the Lord.

The Blessing (Mt.14:18-20): Jesus performs a miracle with 5 fish and 2 loaves of bread. He takes the little that is available and blesses, breaks, and distributes to feed the five thousand.

It's interesting to note that the disciples initially wanted to send the people away. They considered, like many of us, what was lacking, instead of what God had the ability to supply. However, rather than agree with their assessment of the situation, Jesus shares a Word of instruction, which they follow, and the results exceed their expectations.

Through these two examples, Jesus shows us that we do not have to toil or labor in our own might in order to produce. God's Word is sufficient to sustain and produce, if we obey His instructions.

Eve

The Judgment (Gen. 3:16-17): She will have sorrow in conception and childbirth; and her desire will be for her husband.

The Blessing – Childbirth (Luke 1:26-35): Jesus was working in Mary's womb to bless and bring great joy to an experience that was supposed to be sorrowful.

The Blessing - Husband (John 4): This passage recounts Jesus' encounter with the woman at the well. During their conversation, the Lord shifts the Samaritan woman's focus from the natural to the spiritual, in contrast to the devil who shifted Eve's focus from the spiritual to the natural. The woman who admittedly had five husbands would now desire Jesus, our Bridegroom.

Jesus' meeting with the Samaritan woman restores her position, reputation, credibility, and power as a woman. Many would come to Jesus as a result of her testimony.

Adam and Eve

The Judgment (Gen. 3:19): Because of sin, death entered into the world.

The Blessing (Rev. 1:17-18, John 1:1, Mt. 27:52): Jesus has absolute power and victory over death and hades. We witness His power over death, through the resurrection of Lazarus, Jairus' daughter, and

Peter's mother. He further demonstrates His power through His own death and resurrection. The earth shook, graves were opened, and many of the saints who died earlier were raised from the dead (Mt. 27:52). Finally, His resurrection also assures us of a future resurrection for those who die in Him.

I Thessalonians 4: 13-18 *But I do not want you to be ignorant, brethren, concerning those who have fallen asleep, lest you sorrow as others who have no hope. For if we believe that Jesus died and rose again, even so God will bring with Him those who sleep in Jesus. For this we say to you by the word of the Lord, that we who are alive and remain until the coming of the Lord will by no means precede those who are asleep. For the Lord Himself will descend from heaven with a shout, with the voice of an archangel, and with the trumpet of God. And the dead in Christ will rise first. Then we who are alive and remain shall be caught up together with them in the clouds to meet the Lord in the air. And thus we shall always be with the Lord. Therefore comfort one another with these words.*

The Judgment (Gen. 3:24): Man was evicted from the Garden and denied access to the Tree of Life.

The Blessing (John 20): Jesus appears in the Garden after His resurrection, symbolizing that the Garden is now accessible through Him. He's the only way for us to gain entry back into the Father's house.

Back to the Garden of Eden

As a result of the redemptive work of Jesus Christ, we can once again access all that God originally purposed for us in the Garden. With that in mind, let us return to the Garden of Eden and examine what was restored.

1. Restored Us to the Image and Likeness of God

In the image and likeness of God, man was created. Adam and Eve were a reflection of God Himself. However, sin marred the image of man, disrupted our DNA, and caused us to change from that which was incorruptible to corruptible. However, through Jesus, we can be born again into a new man and receive the promise of a glorified body.

***2 Cor. 5:17** Therefore, if anyone is in Christ, he is a new creation; old things have passed away; behold, all things have become new.*

Phil 3:20 – 21 *For our citizenship is in heaven, from which we also eagerly wait for the Savior, the Lord Jesus Christ, who will transform our lowly body that it may be conformed to His glorious body, according to the working by which He is able even to subdue all things to Himself.*

2. Restored Our Sonship

Sin came to separate us from God, but Jesus came to reconcile us back to the Father.

John 1:12-13 *But as many as received Him, to them He gave the right to become children of God, to those who believe in His name: who were born, not of blood, nor of the will of the flesh, nor of the will of man, but of God.*

We are now joint heirs with Christ (Rom. 5:17) and seated in heavenly places with Him (Eph. 2:6).

3. Restored Dominion Over Sin

As a consequence of sin, man was subjected to it. Christ came to free us from sin and give us victory over it.

Romans 6:4-14 *For sin shall not have dominion over you: for ye are not under the law, but under grace.*

Galatians 3:13-14 *Christ has redeemed us from the curse of the law, having become a curse for us (for it is written, "Cursed is everyone who hangs on a tree"), that the blessing of Abraham might come upon the Gentiles in Christ Jesus, that we might receive the promise of the Spirit through faith.*

4. Restored Power Over the Kingdom of Darkness

Jesus has given us power over the kingdom of darkness.

Luke 10:19 *Behold, I give unto you power to tread on serpents and scorpions, and over all the power of the enemy: and nothing shall by any means hurt you.*

5. Restored Us to God's Rest

The position Adam occupied before the fall was one of rest. It was not necessary to toil, since God Himself provided everything that Adam needed and gave His creation the ability to reproduce after its own kind. Adam simply had to follow God's instructions to cultivate and care for the Garden (Gen. 2:15). By failing to follow God's instructions, man transitioned from a place of eternal rest to toil, from working within God's finished work to producing with his own hands. Nevertheless, thanks to God, through our faith in Jesus Christ, we are now able to re-enter into His rest.

Hebrews 4:9-10 *There remains therefore a rest for the people of God. For he who has entered His rest has himself also ceased from his works as God did from His.*

6. Restored Us to Eternal Life

As a result of the fall, death entered the world and passed unto all men (Rom. 5:12). However, Jesus became the propitiation for our sins and now through Him we have access to eternal life.

John 3:16-17 *For God so loved the world that He gave His only begotten Son, that whoever believes in Him should not perish but have everlasting life. For God did not send His Son into the world to condemn the world, but that the world through Him might be saved.*

Chapter 7

Jesus is The End to Our Beginning
All Things New

Jesus is the end to our beginning. He fully satisfied the penalty for sin on the cross and ushered in a new beginning for man. From death to life, from judgement to redemption, from separation to reconciliation, from strangers to sons, from toil to rest, that which Adam and Eve lost is now restored through Jesus Christ.

All Things New

In order to embrace the new life available to us through Christ Jesus, we must be willing to let go of the old. God is ready to make all things new for us. He wants us to experience the blessings of sonship. He did not send Jesus to condemn the world, on the contrary, He came that the world might be saved through Him (John 3:17). The walls of judgment are turned down. So as many as would believe, can experience the fullness of God, His blessings, and newness of life in Him.

> **"And He said to me, "It is done! I am the Alpha and the Omega, the Beginning and the End. I will give of the fountain of the water of life freely to him who thirsts. He who overcomes shall inherit all things, and I will be his God and he shall be My son." – Revelations 21:6-7**

Reflections II

Life Application

1. Why is it important for God to affirm us in our identity?

2. Find scriptures that speak to who God says you are in Him and write them down.

3. Reflect on the ways in which you have experienced the redemptive, restorative, and reconciling work of Christ in your own life.

4. What personal revelation did God share with you in the reading of this book?

2 Peter 3:9 NKJV *The Lord is not slack concerning His promise, as some count slackness, but is longsuffering toward us, not willing that any should perish but that all should come to repentance.*

If you have not embraced God's new beginning for your life, it's not too late to do so. If you embraced your new beginning, but got off course, there's no time like the present to return to the Father. He counted you worthy of redemption having knowledge of the choices that you would make, even when they were contrary to His plan for you. **His plan is still available to you.** Simply repent and ask God for forgiveness and the power to live a life that pleases Him. Ask Him to direct you to a local fellowship or church where His presence reigns, the truth of His Word is ministered, and you can grow in your relationship with Him. Today is the start of a new life in Christ. Trust God to guide, help, and lead you by His Holy Spirit every step of the way.

Acts 2:38-39 NKJV *Then Peter said to them, "Repent, and let every one of you be baptized in the name of Jesus Christ for the remission of sins; and you shall receive the gift of the Holy Spirit. ³⁹ For the promise is for you and for your children and for all who are far off, everyone whom the Lord our God calls to himself."*

THANK GOD FOR A NEW BEGINNING

CONTACT AUTHOR

We'd Love to Hear From You

If *The End to Our Beginning* has blessed or inspired you in any way, we invite you to share your testimony. Your story may encourage someone else on their own journey of faith.

You can connect with **Chawanda Allen** through her author page at:

Because There's More Publishing
Scan the QR code below or visit:
becausetheresmorepublishing.com

Books by Chawanda Allen

- The End to Our Beginning

More books are coming soon! Stay connected for future releases and updates on what God is doing through BTMP.

www.ingramcontent.com/pod-product-compliance
Lightning Source LLC
Chambersburg PA
CBHW070303100426
42743CB00011B/2319